The ACID RAIN HAZARD

BY JUDITH WOODBURN

ENVIRONMENT ALERT!

Gareth Stevens Publishing
MILWAUKEE

For a free color catalog describing Gareth Stevens' list of high-quality books, call 1-800-341-3569 (USA) or 1-800-461-9120 (Canada).

Library of Congress Cataloging-in-Publication Data

Woodburn, Judith, 1959-
      The acid rain hazard / Judith Woodburn.
         p. cm. — (Environment alert!)
      Includes bibliographical references and index.
      Summary: Discusses the causes of acid rain and how it damages the environment, and
   suggests ways to prevent and reverse acid rain and its effects.
      ISBN 0-8368-0697-2
      1. Acid rain—Environmental aspects—Juvenile literature. 2. Air—Pollution—Juvenile
   literature. [1. Acid rain—Environmental aspects. 2. Air—Pollution. 3. Pollution.]
   I. Title. II. Series.
   TD195.44.W68 1991
   363.78'88—dc20   91-50340

Edited, designed, and produced by
Gareth Stevens Publishing
1555 North RiverCenter Drive, Suite 201
Milwaukee, WI 53212, USA

Picture Credits:

© Walt Anderson/Visuals Unlimited, p. 11; © Frank S. Balthis, p. 21; © W. A.
Banaszewski/Visuals Unlimited, p. 22; © Nigel Blythe/Picture Perfect USA, p. 25
(lower); Sharone Burris, 1991, p. 14; © John C. Coulter/Visuals Unlimited, pp.
14-15 (inset); © Adrian Davies/Bruce Coleman Limited, front cover (inset), title;
Courtesy of Charles Driscoll, pp. 12-13 (upper), p. 13; © Chris Fairclough Colour
Library, pp. 2-3, p. 16; Rick Karpinski/DeWalt & Associates, 1992, pp. 8-9, p. 20;
© Herbert Kranawetter/Bruce Coleman Limited, pp. 26-27; © Link/Visuals
Unlimited, pp. 4-5; © Mike McQueen/IMPACT Photos, p. 25 (upper); Michael
Medynsky/Artisan, 1992, pp. 12-13 (lower); Roger Phillips, 1991, pp. 6-7; © Picture
Perfect USA, p. 5; © Hans Reinhard/Bruce Coleman Limited, cover, pp. 14-15, p.
17; © Stan Ries/International Stock, p. 23; © Scott T. Smith/Picture Perfect USA,
p. 18; Tim Spransy, 1991, pp. 28-29; © Bill Stanton/International Stock, pp. 22-23;
© Norman Owen Tomalin/Bruce Coleman Limited, p. 9; UPI/Bettmann, p. 19;
Keith Ward, 1992, pp.10-11, p. 24.

Map information on pp. 6-7 from *Atlas of the Environment*, New York: Prentice Hall
Press, 1990, pp. 86-87.

Series editor: Patricia Lantier-Sampon
Series designer: Laurie Shock
Book designer: Sabine Beaupré
Picture researcher: Diane Laska
Research editor: Aldemar Hagen

Printed in the United States of America

1 2 3 4 5 6 7 8 9 97 96 95 94 93 92

President

CONTENTS

Words that appear in the glossary are printed in **boldface** type the first
time they appear in the text.

TROUBLE FROM THE SKY

When rain falls to Earth, it looks as clear as glass. But sometimes the rain is not as pure as it looks. In many parts of the world, raindrops carry invisible bits of pollution. When this pollution makes the rain more **acidic** than it should be, it's called **acid rain**. In some places, the rain is as sour as vinegar!

The chemicals in acid rain sometimes make the sky look dark and hazy. And when acid rain falls to Earth, it damages many things. It destroys the paint and metal on cars. It can wear away the surfaces of monuments and buildings, such as the Parthenon in Greece and the Taj Mahal in India.

Acid rain is even more dangerous to plants and animals. In many forests, it has killed older trees and is stopping new ones from growing. Many lakes don't have any fish at all because acid rain has killed them!

People in many countries are trying to stop acid rain. If we don't stop it fast enough, many more forests and lakes will die.

The Parthenon in Greece has lasted 25 centuries, but now it is being destroyed by acid rain.

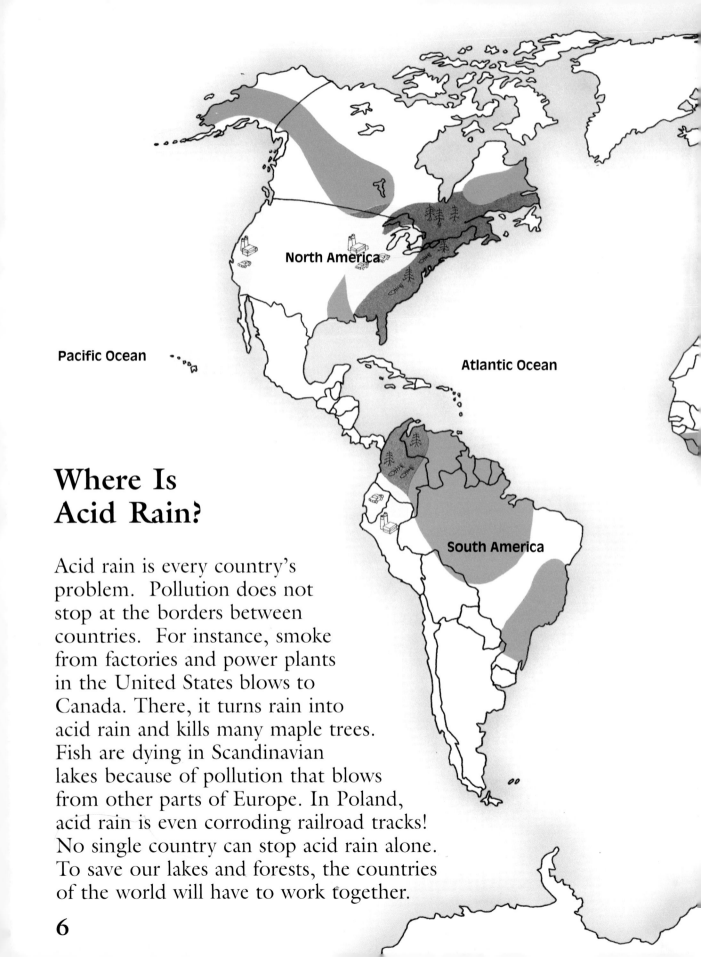

Pacific Ocean

North America

Atlantic Ocean

South America

Where Is Acid Rain?

Acid rain is every country's problem. Pollution does not stop at the borders between countries. For instance, smoke from factories and power plants in the United States blows to Canada. There, it turns rain into acid rain and kills many maple trees. Fish are dying in Scandinavian lakes because of pollution that blows from other parts of Europe. In Poland, acid rain is even corroding railroad tracks! No single country can stop acid rain alone. To save our lakes and forests, the countries of the world will have to work together.

6

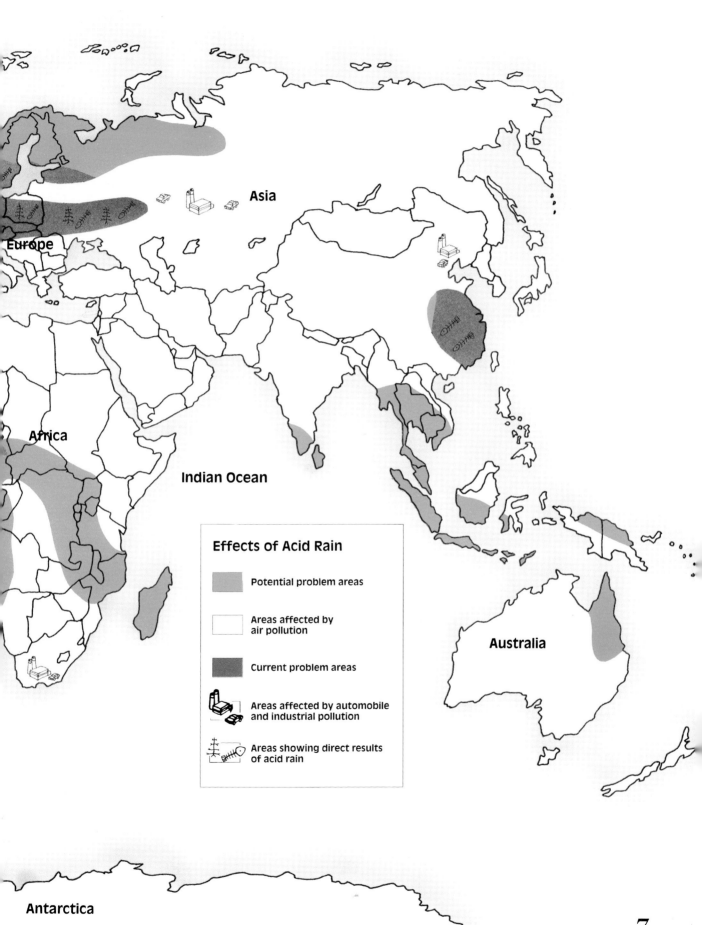

Effects of Acid Rain

Potential problem areas

Areas affected by
air pollution

Current problem areas

Areas affected by automobile
and industrial pollution

Areas showing direct results
of acid rain

Europe

Asia

Africa

Indian Ocean

Australia

Antarctica

7

How Acid Rain Began

To stop acid rain, we need to understand what causes it. Centuries ago, humans learned how to extract coal and oil from the ground and burn them to heat their homes. Today, we get electricity from power plants that burn coal. We use oil to make gasoline, which fuels our cars. All of these inventions help make our lives easier, but they also cause problems. As coal and gasoline burn, they release pollution into the air.

Some of these pollutants are chemicals called **sulfur dioxide** and **nitrogen oxides**. They can float long distances in the wind. As they float, they mix with other chemicals in the air to create acid particles. When this chemical pollution falls to Earth in the form of dry particles, scientists call it **dry deposition**. Or the particles can mix with rain, snow, or fog. Scientists call this **wet deposition**. As a shortcut, most people just call this "acid rain."

Even though acid rain started long ago, scientists are just beginning to understand the problems it causes.

A Statue of a Different Color

A few years ago, people noticed that acid rain was turning the Statue of Liberty in New York City orange-brown. The statue was given a protective coating to help it resist the acids. It is just one of many monuments in the world that have been damaged by acid rain.

This illustration of a modern city landscape shows how pollution created by transportation vehicles, industrial processes, and everyday home life mixes with rain and snow to form acid rain. This acid rain then spills over into the surrounding countryside and is carried to other parts of the Earth by strong winds. The acid rain is absorbed by plant and animal life, finally finding its way into the soil and the natural water supply.

What Is an Acid?

An acid is a substance that has a sour, tangy taste. Many substances in your house are acidic, such as lemon juice and vinegar. They taste tart. Many other common substances are just the opposite, or **alkaline**. Baking soda is alkaline. It has a soapy, bitter flavor. Distilled water is neither acid nor alkaline. It's **neutral** and has no flavor.

Normal rain is usually slightly acidic. The only way to find out if the rain has gotten too acidic is to test the soil and lake water. To help them understand acid rain better, scientists all over the world are collecting samples of water and soil to test for acidity.

The pH Scale

Scientists measure the degree and strength of the acid present in different substances by using the **pH scale**. This special system of measurement moves on a scale of numbers that range from 0 to 14. The lower the number, the stronger the acid content. Therefore, acids have low pH numbers. Lemon juice, for example, is much more acidic than distilled water, so it has a lower number.

Right: Rain provides moisture to a woolly mullein wildflower in Oregon.

pH Scale

1	2	3	4
	lemon juice	vinegar	
		← acid rain →	

Acid

| 5 | 6 | 7 | 8 | 9 | 10 | 11 | 12 | 13 | 14 |

coffee · normal rain · distilled water · baking soda

Neutral .... Alkali

FACT FILE
The Adirondacks:
A Land of Dead Lakes

Woods Lake is one of thousands of lakes in the Adirondack Mountains of New York State. Many years ago, anglers caught plenty of fish on Woods Lake. But for a while, there were no fish to catch!

Over the years, acid rain built up in Woods Lake. The lake became too acidic for fish to live in. Many other lake creatures, such as snails and tadpoles, could not live there either. Because of too much acid in the lake, scientists said it had been "acidified."

Over 300 other lakes in the Adirondack Mountains lost their fish, too. One way to de-acidify these lakes was with truckloads of **lime**. After a lake is limed, wildlife slowly returns. But liming is expensive and may cause other problems in the lake. Scientists decided to de-acidify Woods Lake in spite of the problems involved, and small fish stocked in the lake have grown and are now reproducing.

golden shiner

rainbow trout

12

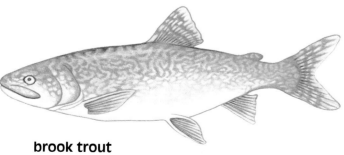

brook trout

Above: Woods Lake looks clear and pretty. The damage caused by acid rain is beneath the surface.

Inset: A helicopter dumps lime, an alkaline substance, into Woods Lake.

Left: These freshwater fish were once common in lakes of the Adirondack Mountains.

FACT FILE
The Disappearing Black Forest

The Black Forest in the mountains of southwestern Germany was once covered with evergreen trees. Years ago, acid rain began making the needles of many of these trees turn yellow and fall to the forest floor. Soon, many of the trees died. Without their needles, the trees looked like skeletons. The German people sadly called this sickness *Waldsterben*, or "forest death."

Some people think that cars traveling on high-speed German highways, called *autobahns*, cause the acid rain. Cars on the autobahns speeding well over 100 miles per hour (160 kph) burn large amounts of gas and create extra pollution.

Strong winds blow the pollution to the Black Forest, where it turns to acid rain and falls on the trees and ground. But the acid rain does not kill the trees directly. Instead, it prevents the evergreens from getting the **nutrients** they need from the soil. This weakens the trees, and they cannot fight off deadly diseases.

A section of the Black Forest damaged by acid rain. By the time Germans realized their forests were in trouble, much of the damage had already been done. Even healthy-looking trees (inset) may be sick.

15

Today, the people of Germany are working hard to save their forests. Many want stricter speed limits on the autobahns to make cars slow down. Slower-moving cars burn less gasoline and create less pollution. New laws are also making Germany's factories and power plants cut back on the pollution that causes acid rain. Germany's neighboring countries have promised to cut back on air pollution, too.

Foresters can protect some younger trees by giving them extra food, or fertilizer. Unfortunately, this will not keep all the trees from getting sick. The only real hope is to work at cleaning up the air.

Opposite: Trees in Germany's Black Forest are going bald from the effects of acid rain.

Below: Cars on a German autobahn, which has no speed limits, create huge amounts of pollution.

STOPPING ACID RAIN

Kicking the Coal Habit

Coal-burning power plants are the main source of the air pollution that causes acid rain. Every year, the power plants of the world puff more than 66 million tons of sulfur dioxides into the air through their smokestacks.

Many years ago, the air around the power plants was extremely polluted. Then, the power companies had an idea. They made their smokestacks much taller — as tall as skyscrapers — and the smoke just blew away with the wind. But this didn't really solve the problem. The wind just blew the pollution into somebody else's air.

To stop acid rain, power plants need to cut back on pollution, not just send it farther away. One way to do this is to clean the smoke before it comes out of the smokestacks. This is done with machines called **scrubbers.** In many countries, such as Japan, all new power plants and factories must be built with scrubbers. Many old plants, however, do not have scrubbers yet because they are costly to install.

London's Killer Smog

When too much pollution collects in the air, it can be dangerous. In 1952, weather patterns over the city of London prevented smoke from coal fires from blowing away. The smoke mixed with fog. Londoners invented a new word for it: **smog**. The thick smog made breathing almost impossible. More than 4,000 people suffocated from breathing in this polluted air.

Opposite: A coal-burning power plant in Wyoming. The acid-causing particles in its smoke can travel for thousands of miles.

Power plants can use special coal that is not so dirty when it burns. We can also kick the coal habit by finding cleaner ways to generate electricity. Instead of burning coal, some power plants make electricity from fast-moving water. Some even make electricity from the force of the wind!

Unfortunately, many power companies don't want to make these changes. They complain that it would cost too much. But in the long run, saving forests and lakes from acid rain may cost even more.

Opposite: In Palm Springs, California, there are thousands of windmills in "wind farms." The swiftly rotating blades power generators that produce electricity.

Below: There are many ways of generating electricity, such as wind power; hydroelectric dams, which generate power from the force of moving water; nuclear power, which harnesses the powerful force of splitting atoms; solar panels, which convert energy from the sun into electricity; and wave power from the sea.

Clearing the Smog from Cars and Trucks

Big power plants with enormous smokestacks aren't the only cause of acid rain. For instance, the tail pipe on your family's car acts like a tiny smokestack. Tail pipes pump *tons* of pollutants into the air every year!

One kind of pollution from cars is nitrogen oxide. Like the sulfur dioxides from power plants, nitrogen oxide helps cause acid rain.

In many countries, new cars must use **unleaded fuel** and have special filters, called **catalytic converters**, to reduce pollution. Despite these safeguards, the problem just keeps getting worse because more people are driving cars and trucks than ever before.

Above: The world is experiencing an automobile population explosion. There are eight times as many cars on the road today as there were just 40 years ago.

Opposite: Large industrial trucks are a major source of highway air pollution.

The Polluter in Your Garage

Every year, the average family car gives off 66 pounds (30 kg) of nitrogen oxide. With 400 million cars on the road worldwide, the pollution problem just keeps getting worse.

23

To stop acid rain, cars and trucks need to gobble less fuel. Automakers can help by making cars that go farther on less gas. Each of us can help by cutting back on the number of trips we take by car. We can carpool instead of riding alone.

Instead of using gasoline power to ride in cars, we can use muscle power. We can walk or ride our bicycles. Or we can hop on a bus or train. Since buses and trains carry many people at once, they waste less fuel. Some cities are building new train lines to help cut back on pollution from cars and trucks.

The chart below shows that using public transportation is more environment-friendly and fuel-efficient than owning and using individual vehicles.

Transportation and the Atmosphere	# of passengers per automobile, bus, or train car	# of miles (km) per person per gallon of fuel
	🚶	22 (35 km)
	 🚶🚶🚶🚶	89 (143 km)
	 🚶 × 40	124 (200 km)
	 🚶 × 64	136 (219 km)

Above: Pedestrians on the London Bridge.

Right: The "Underground" in London is one of many modern train systems serving cities all over the world.

The Big Debate

Many people agree that acid rain must be stopped. But there is still a lot of debate about how to do it — and who should pay for it. Power companies and automakers say they need more proof of where acid rain comes from before they will agree to spend money on solutions to the problem. And when acid rain crosses international borders, countries debate about who is responsible.

Countries suffering from acid rain have no way to force their neighbors to clean up the air. The only answer is for nations to cooperate. Sweden, where many lakes are dying from acidification, has convinced some countries to cooperate. These countries have all signed an agreement to reduce their pollution by about one-third. This means strong efforts must be made to clean factory smoke before it mixes with outside air, lower the speed limits on highways, and use cleaner sources of energy. And it can be done! Already, Japan has cut its sulfur dioxide pollution by more than half.

To save lakes and forests from acid rain, more countries must cooperate. If they wait too long, it may be too late.

Lake Garda in Italy is a beautiful place to visit. With care, we can preserve our air quality so that all lakes and trees stay healthy.

RESEARCH ACTIVITIES

1. Find out about acidity.

Ask your teacher for a few strips of pH test paper. This paper turns reddish-pink in an acidic substance and blue in an alkaline substance. Pour about one inch (2.54 cm) of distilled water into a cup. Dip one edge of the paper in the water. Does the paper change color?

Now pour one inch (2.54 cm) of vinegar into a cup. Dip the test paper in the vinegar. What color is the paper now? Is vinegar acid or alkaline? Test other liquids for acidity, such as milk, orange juice, soapy water, saltwater, and tea. Think of other liquids that you can test. Which ones are acidic and which are alkaline?

2. Test your rain for acidity.

When it rains, place a clean cup outside and collect about an inch (2.54 cm) of rain. Dip a fresh strip of pH test paper in the rainwater. What color is the paper? Is the rainwater alkaline or acidic?

If the rain has an acidic quality, take a walking tour of your city or the area around your home to see if anything has been damaged by acid rain. How do monuments or statues look? How about buildings made out of different materials? Record your observations and try to decide if some substances are more affected by acid rain than others.

3. Find out about plants and acidic conditions.

Wet a square of cloth (a clean rag will do) with water. Sprinkle some radish or alfalfa seeds on the wet cloth. Carefully line the inside of a clean glass jar with the cloth so that the seeds are pressed against the glass. Cover the top of the jar with some plastic wrap and fasten with a rubber band.

Now wet another square of cloth with vinegar instead of water. Follow the same steps as above with another clean glass jar.

Label both jars and place them in the dark until the seeds start to sprout. Then move them into the light. Caution: Don't put them right next to a window where they will get too much light!

If the cloths dry out, add more water or vinegar. Observe the seeds over the next few weeks. Does one jar of seeds grow better than the other?

Things You Can Do to Help

The following activities will help prevent acid rain. Try to involve your friends, family, and classmates in your conservation efforts.

1. **Put your family car on a gasoline diet — drive less.** Ask your parents to help you form a school carpool with friends who live nearby. Better yet, walk or ride your bicycle to school and ask your friends to do the same.

2. **Call your local electric company and ask about ways to conserve electricity in your home.** Also, try not to buy things if you don't really need them. Many things made in factories use lots of electricity.

3. **Write to your local and national government representatives.** Ask them to support laws that promote better mass transit and reduce air pollution.

4. **Form a compost pile in the backyard of your home out of the organic garbage your family produces.** How can the members of your family use this pile? Be sure not to burn any of the garbage around your home. Some communities have laws or ordinances against burning piles of garbage. Find out what the laws are in your own community.

Places to Write for More Information

The following organizations can tell you more about acid rain. When you write to them for more information, be specific about what you want to know.

National Clean Air
    Coalition
530 7th Street S.E.
Washington, D.C. 20003

The Acid Rain
    Foundation, Inc.
1410 Varsity Drive
Raleigh, NC 27606

Pollution Probe
12 Madison Avenue
Toronto, Ontario
M5R 2S1

More Books to Read

Acid Rain, by John Baines (Steck-Vaughn)
Conserving the Atmosphere, by John Baines (Steck-Vaughn)
Ecology: Our Living Planet, by Paula Hogan (Gareth Stevens)
Pollution, by Geraldine and Harold Woods (Franklin Watts)

Glossary

acidic — sour-tasting or tart and measuring low on the pH scale.

acid rain — rain or snow that has mixed with air pollution and causes the death of lakes and forests.

alkaline — bitter-tasting and measuring high on the pH scale.

catalytic converters — special filters on cars and trucks that help remove pollution from their exhaust.

dry deposition — the falling to Earth of dry particles of pollution.

lime — an alkaline powder dug from the ground and used to help neutralize the water in acidified lakes.

neutral — when a substance is neither acid or alkaline, such as distilled water.

nitrogen oxides — a family of gases that are produced from burning gasoline.

nutrients — substances in food and soil that help plants and animals grow.

pH scale — a scale measuring from 0 to 14 that shows how acidic or alkaline a substance is. The lower the number, the more acidic the substance is. The higher the number, the more alkaline it is.

scrubbers — special filters on smokestacks that help remove sulfur dioxide from the smoke.

smog — a combination of the words *smoke* and *fog* used to describe fog that has become polluted with smoke.

sulfur dioxide — a polluting gas created when coal is burned.

unleaded fuel — gasoline from which lead, a toxic metal, has been removed.

wet deposition — the falling of small particles of pollution to Earth after they have mixed with rain, snow, or fog.

Index